HAL•LEONARD

GUITAR

PLAY-ALONG

BRUNO MARS

VOL. 180

CONTENTS

Cover photo © Shirlaine Forrest/Getty Images

ISBN 978-1-4803-9498-8

HAL•LEONARD®
CORPORATION
7777 W. BLUEMOUND RD. P.O. BOX 13819 MILWAUKEE, WI 53213

In Australia Contact:
Hal Leonard Australia Pty. Ltd.
4 Lentara Court
Cheltenham, Victoria, 3192 Australia
Email: ausadmin@halleonard.com.au

Visit Hal Leonard Online at
www.halleonard.com

Count on Me

Words and Music by Bruno Mars, Ari Levine and Philip Lawrence

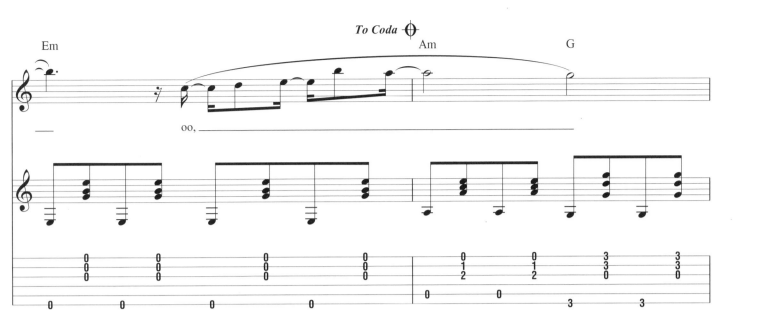

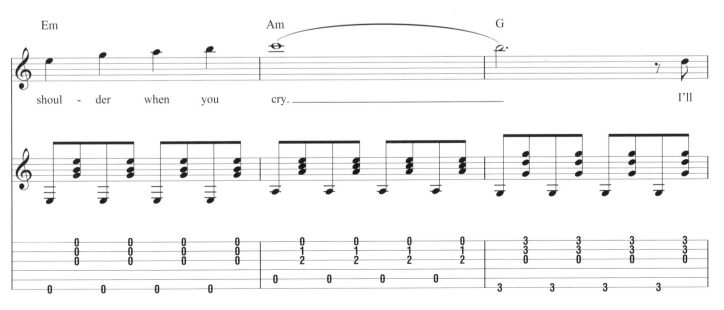

D.S. al Coda

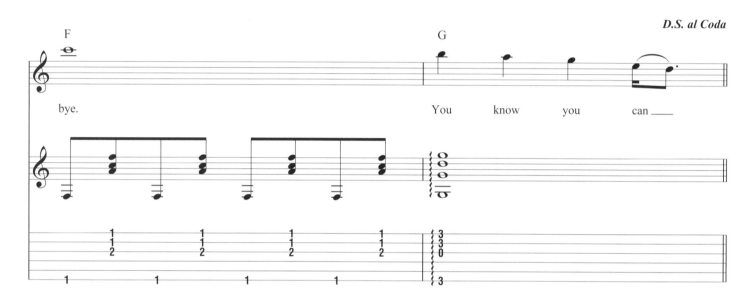

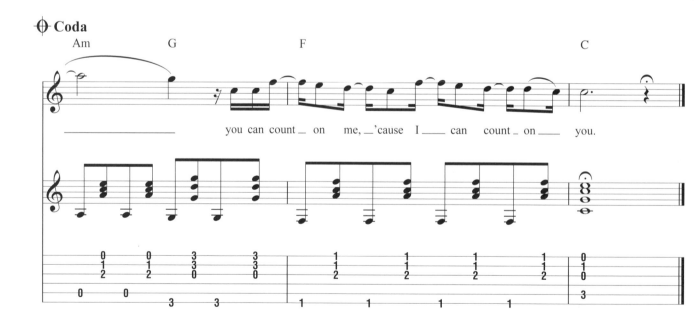

Additional Lyrics

2. If you're tossin' and you're turnin' and you just can't fall asleep,
   I'll sing a song beside you.
   And if you ever forget how much you really mean to me,
   Ev'ry day I will remind you.

Grenade

**Words and Music by Bruno Mars, Ari Levine, Philip Lawrence,
Brody Brown, Claude Kelly and Andrew Wyatt**

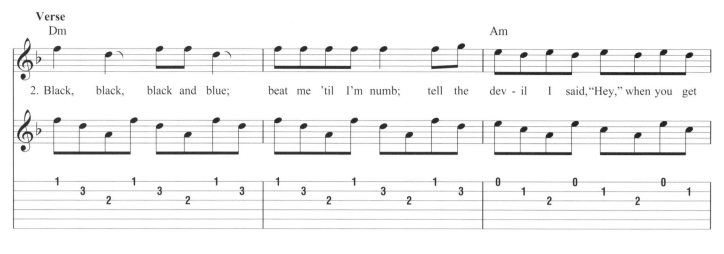

2. Black, black, black and blue; beat me 'til I'm numb; tell the dev - il I said, "Hey," when you get

back to where you're from. Mad wom - an, bad wom - an;

D.S. al Coda

that's just what you are. Yeah, you'll smile — in my face, then rip the brakes out my car.

⊕ Coda

Bridge

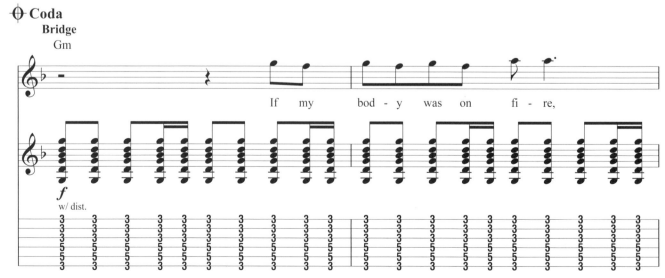

If my bod - y was on fi - re,

f
w/ dist.

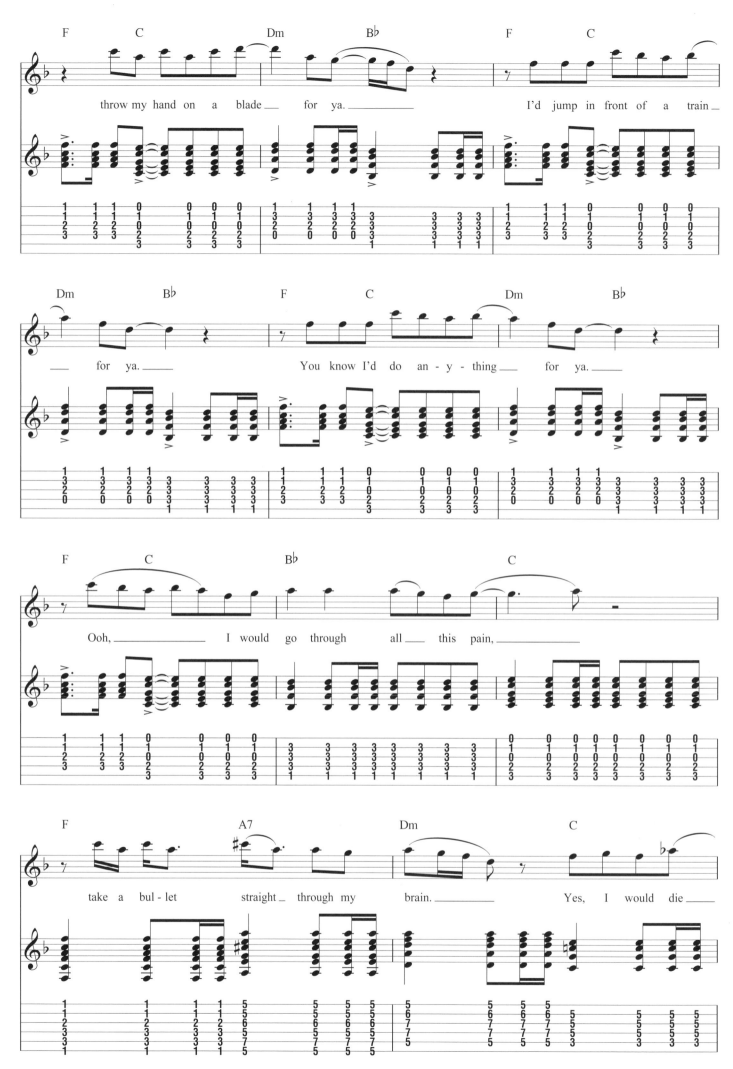

It Will Rain

from the Summit Entertainment film THE TWILIGHT SAGA: BREAKING DAWN - PART 1
Words and Music by Bruno Mars, Philip Lawrence and Ari Levine

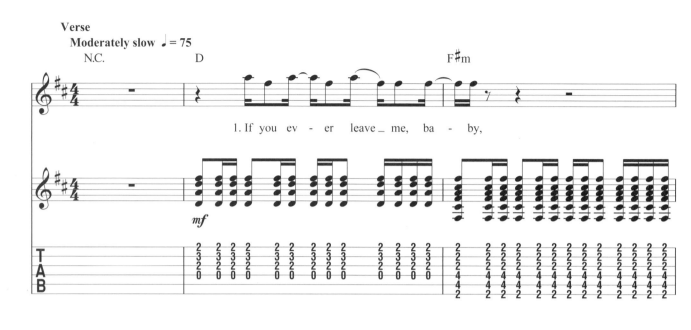

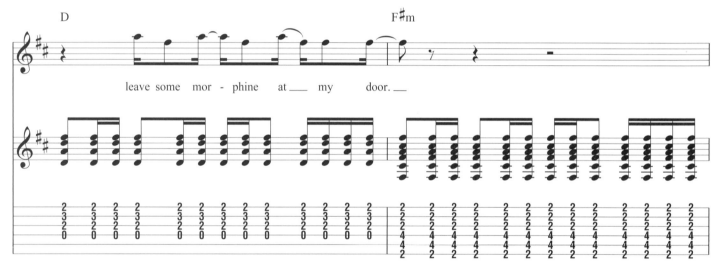

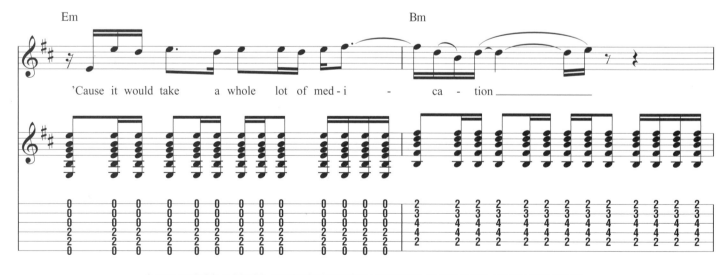

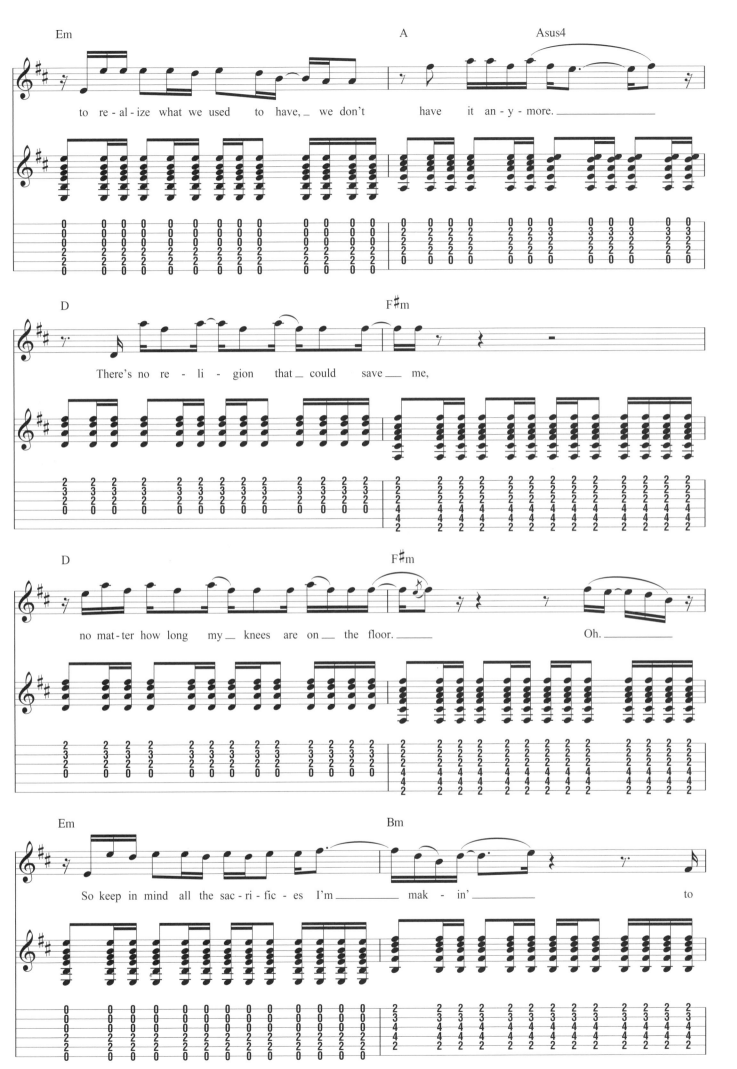

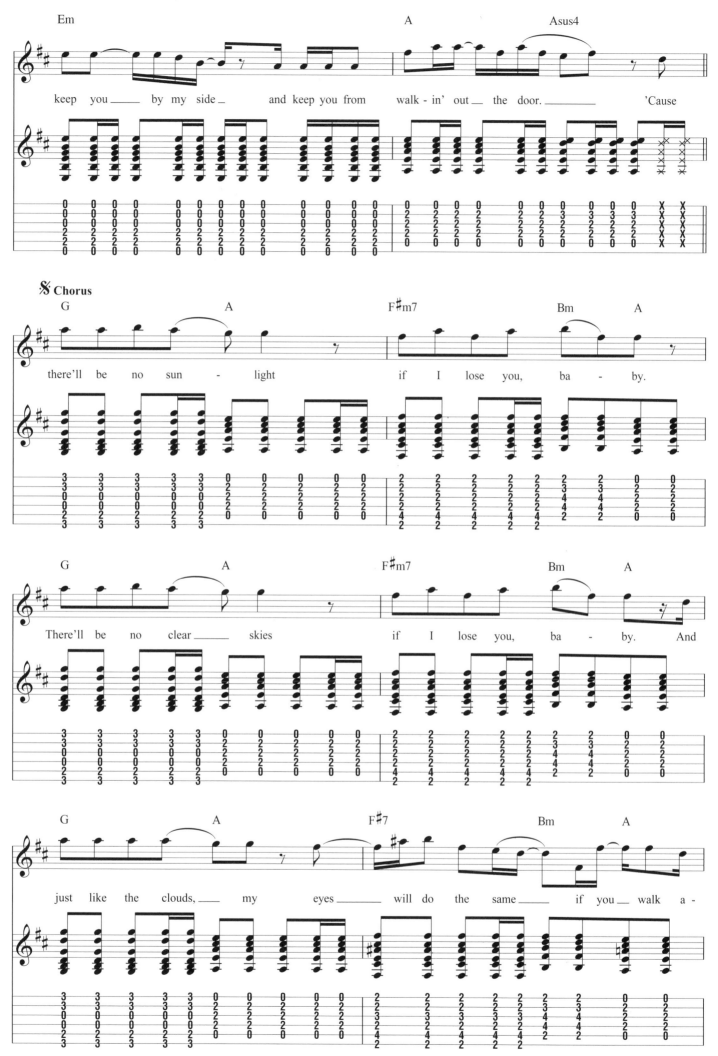

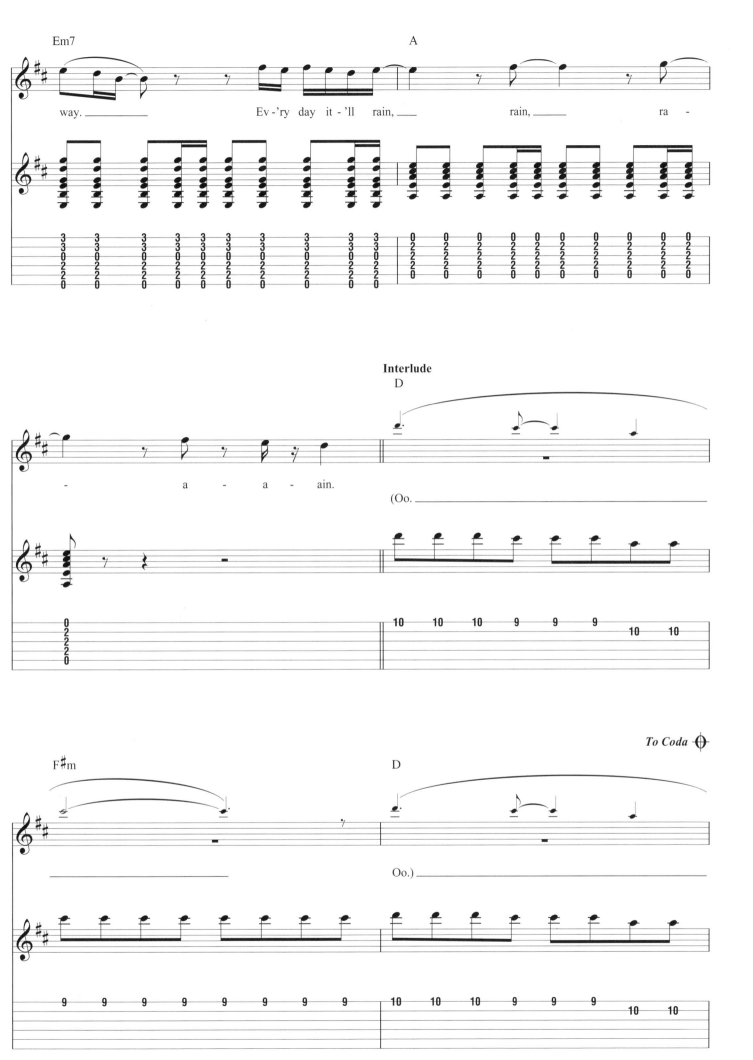

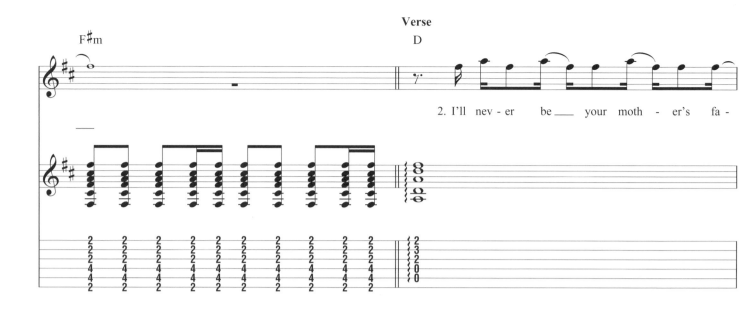

Verse

2. I'll nev - er be ___ your moth - er's fa -

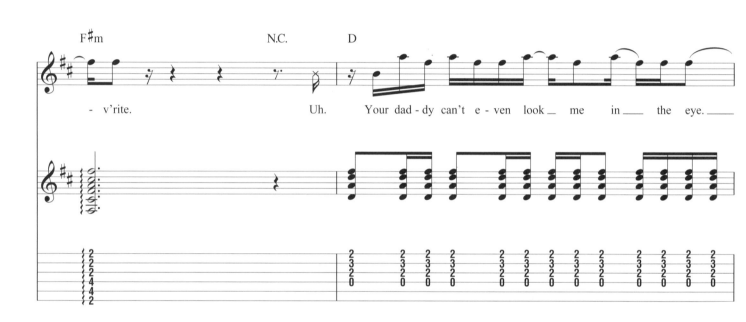

- v'rite.   Uh.   Your dad - dy can't e - ven look ___ me   in ___ the   eye.

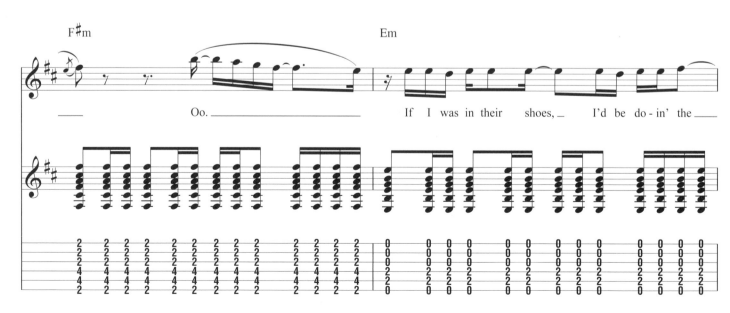

___   Oo. _____   If   I   was in their   shoes, ___   I'd be do - in' the ___

_same _ thing, _____ say-in', "There goes ____ my lit-tle girl, _ walk-in' with that __

___ trou - ble-some _ guy." _____ But they're _ just a-fraid _ of some-thing they _ can't un-_

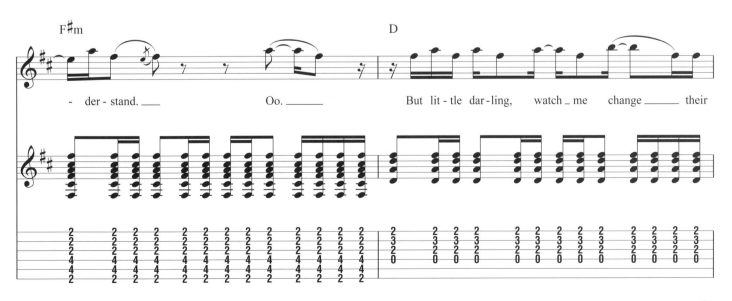

_- der - stand. ___ Oo. ____ But lit-tle dar-ling, watch _ me change ____ their_

minds. ___ Yeah, for you I'll try, ___ I'll try, ___ I'll try, ___ I'll try - y - y, ___

___ and pick up these bro - ken piec - es till ___ I'm bleed - ing if

D.S. al Coda

that -'ll make ___ you mine. _____ 'Cause

✆ Coda

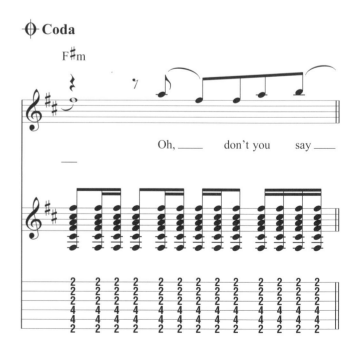

Oh, ___ don't you say ___

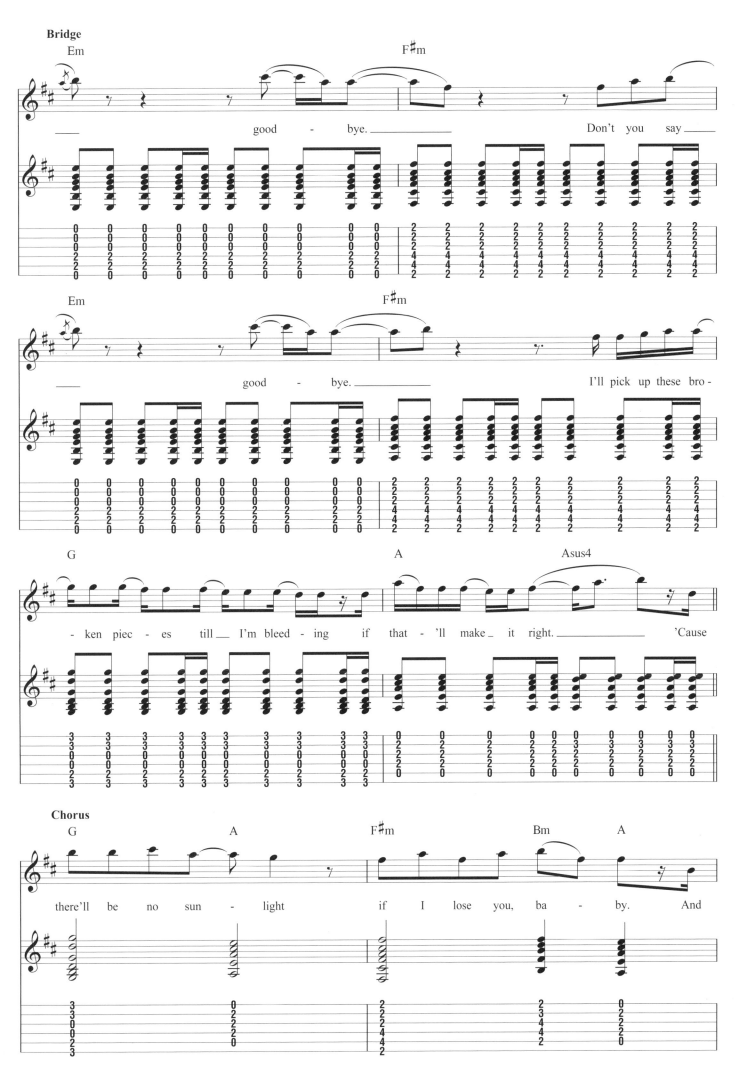

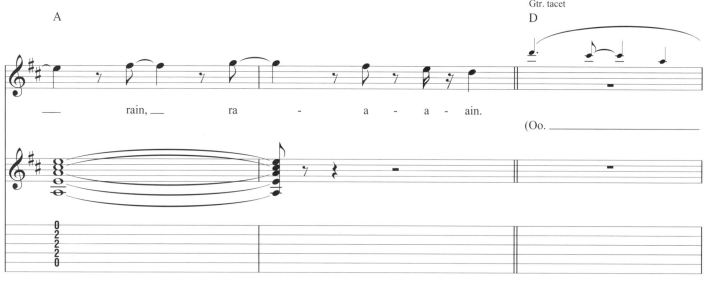

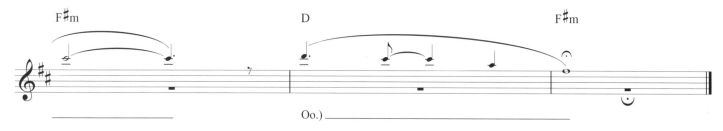

Just the Way You Are

Words and Music by Bruno Mars, Ari Levine, Philip Lawrence, Khari Cain and Khalil Walton

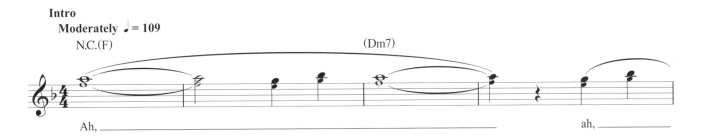

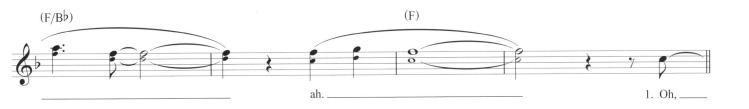

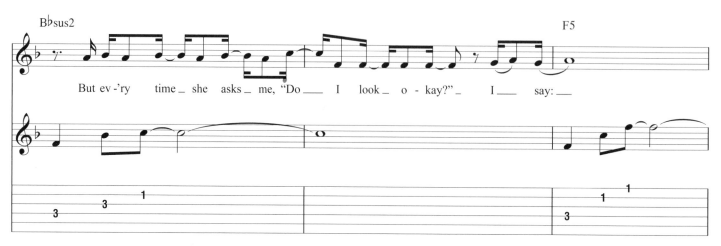

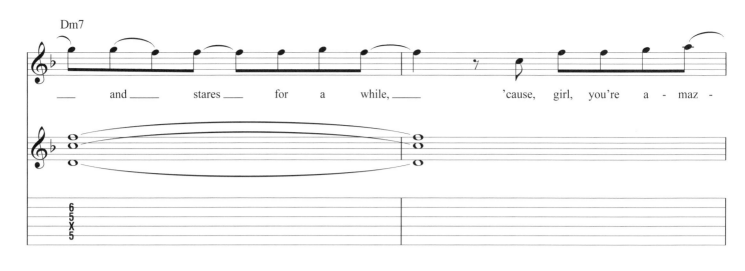

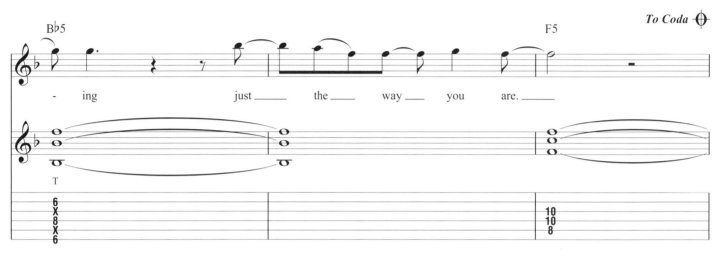

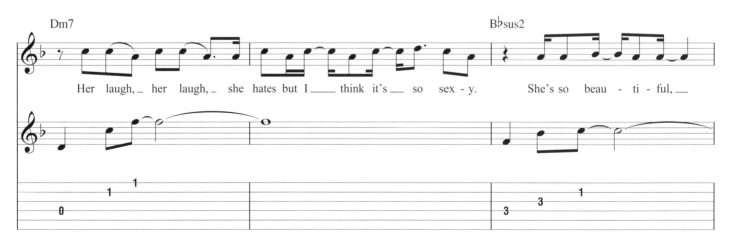

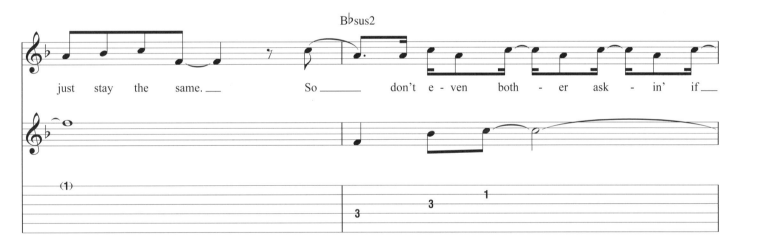

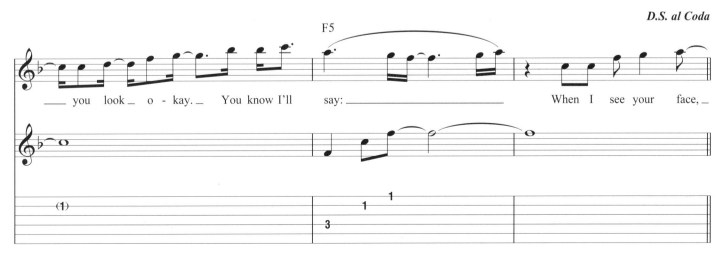

-ing just the way you are.

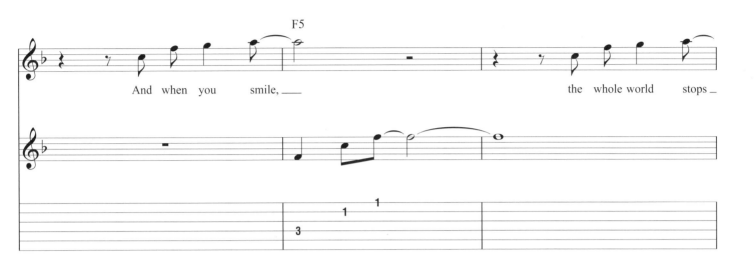

And when you smile, the whole world stops

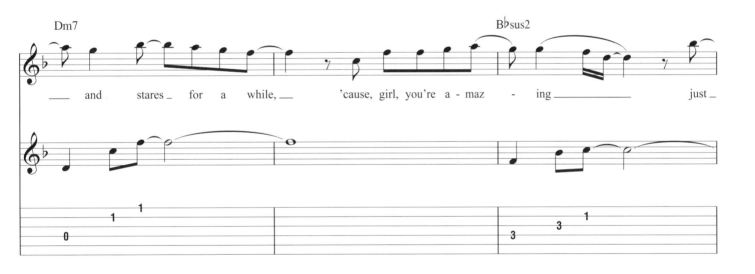

and stares for a while, 'cause, girl, you're a - maz - ing just

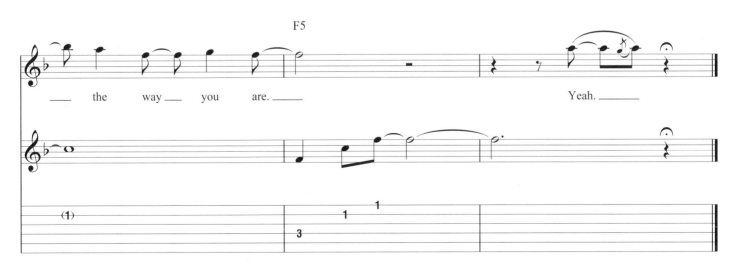

the way you are. Yeah.

The Lazy Song

Words and Music by Bruno Mars, Ari Levine, Philip Lawrence and Keinan Warsame

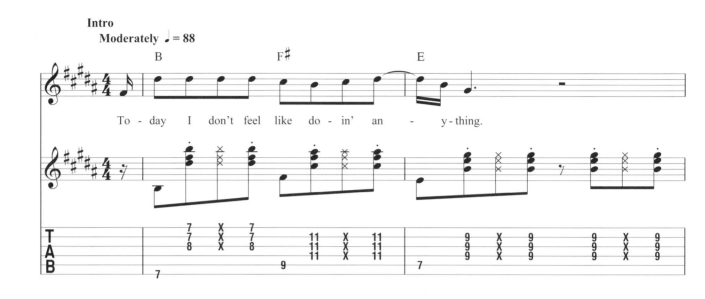

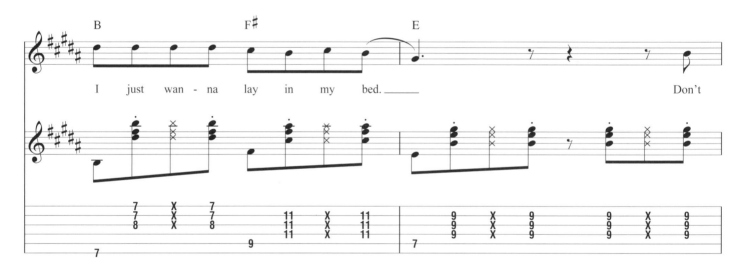

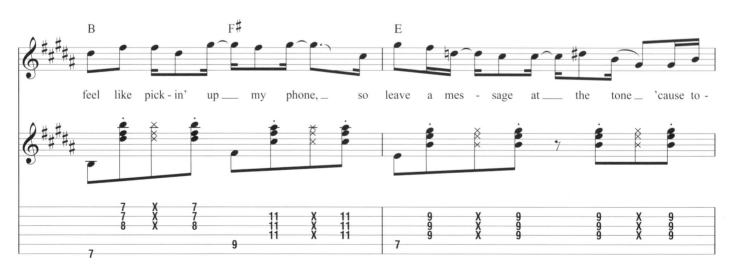

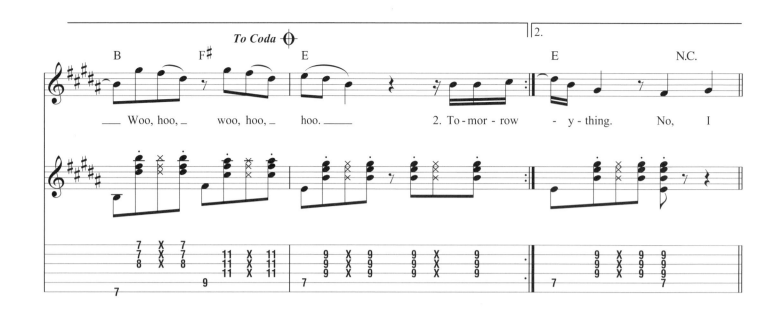

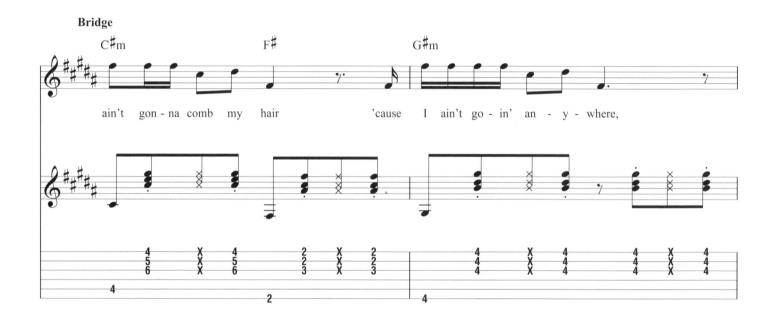

Additional Lyrics

2. Tomorrow I'll wake up, do some P90X,
Meet a really nice girl, have some really nice sex,
And she's gonna scream out, "This is great."
Female (spoken): (Oh, my god, this is great.)
Yeah, I might mess around and get my college degree.
I bet my old man will be so proud of me.
Well, sorry, Pops, you'll just have to wait.

Locked Out of Heaven

Words and Music by Bruno Mars, Ari Levine and Philip Lawrence

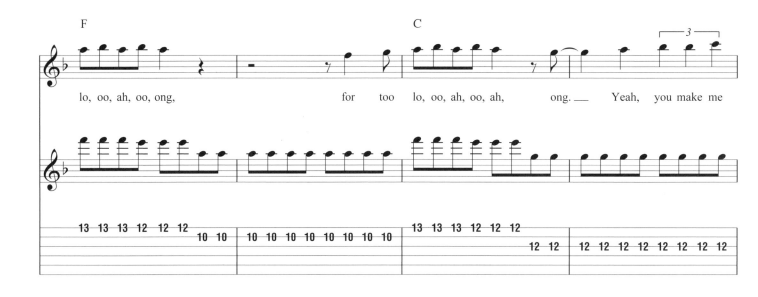

lo, oo, ah, oo, ong,   for too   lo, oo, ah, oo, ah,   ong. ___ Yeah, you make me

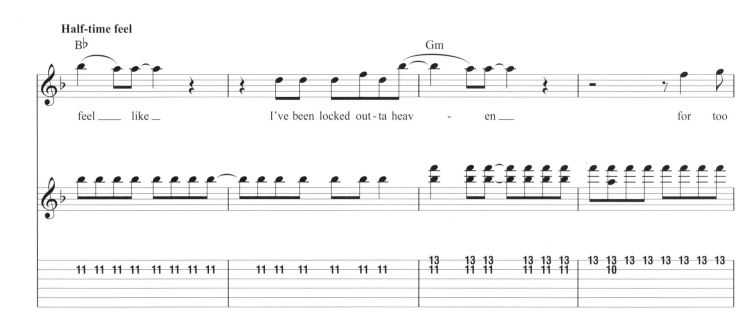

feel ___ like ___   I've been locked out-ta heav   - en ___   for too

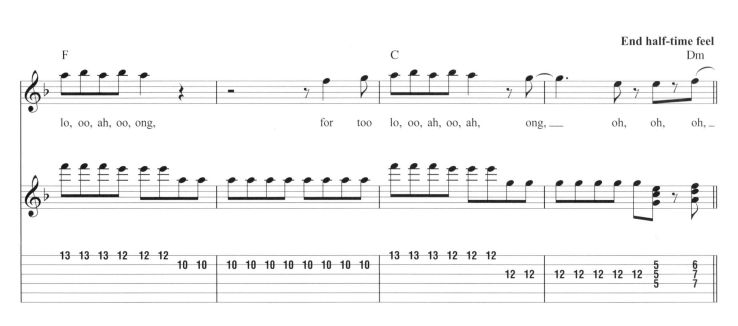

lo, oo, ah, oo, ong,   for too   lo, oo, ah, oo, ah,   ong, ___   oh,   oh,   oh, ___

Outro

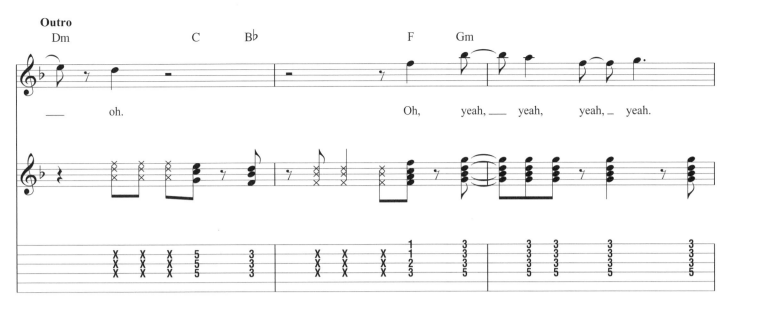

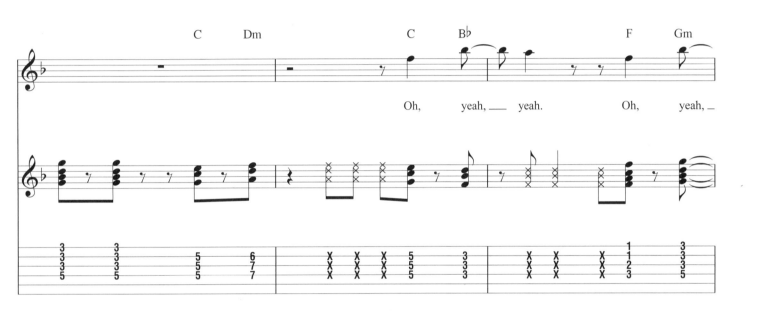

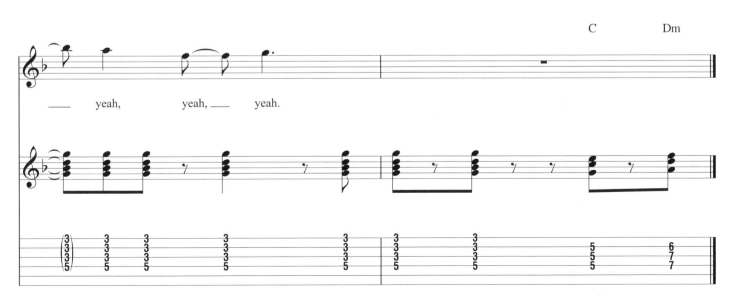

Runaway Baby

Words and Music by Bruno Mars, Ari Levine, Philip Lawrence and Christopher Steven Brown

way. But when I play, I nev-er stay. So ev-'ry

Don't go a-way. Ah, when I play, I nev-er stay.)

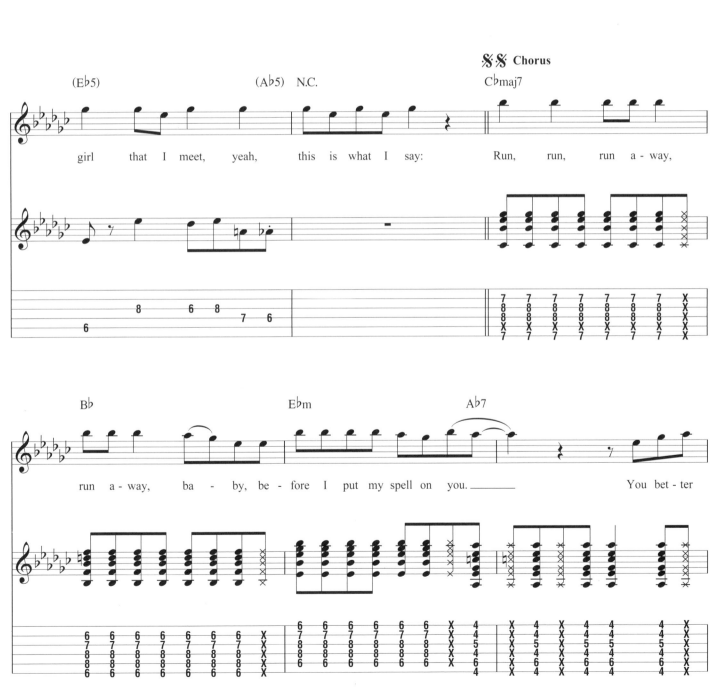

girl that I meet, yeah, this is what I say: Run, run, run a-way,

%% Chorus

run a-way, ba-by, be-fore I put my spell on you._____ You bet-ter

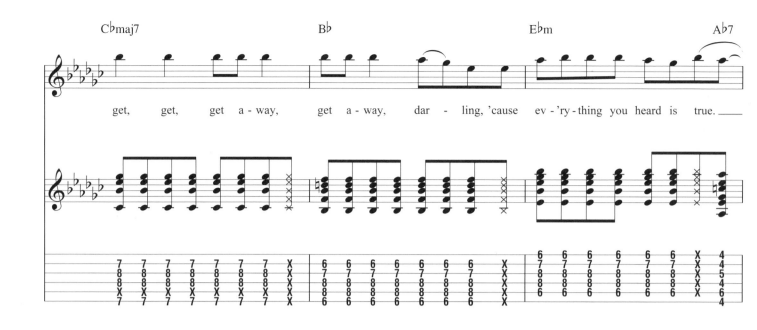

get, get, get a - way, get a - way, dar - ling, 'cause ev - 'ry - thing you heard is true. ___

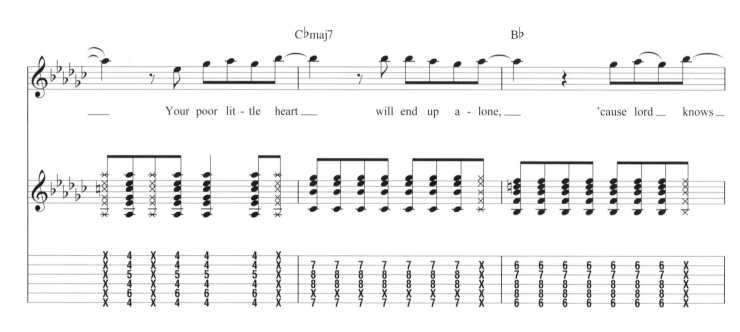

___ Your poor lit - tle heart ___ will end up a - lone, ___ 'cause lord ___ knows ___

To Coda 2

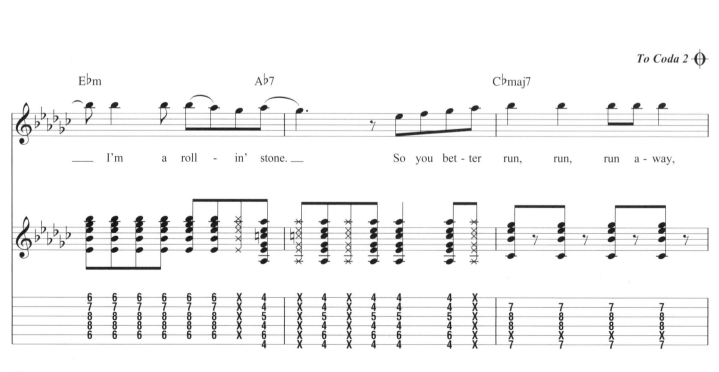

___ I'm a roll - in' stone. ___ So you bet - ter run, run, run a - way,

Interlude

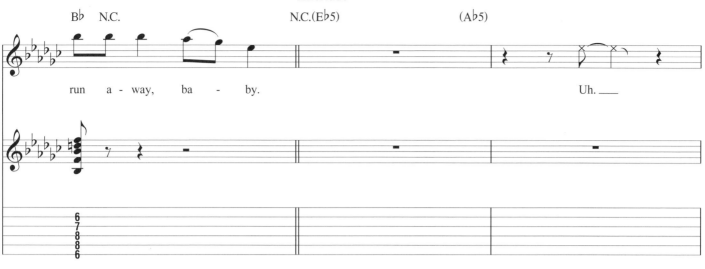

run a - way, ba - by.   Uh. ___

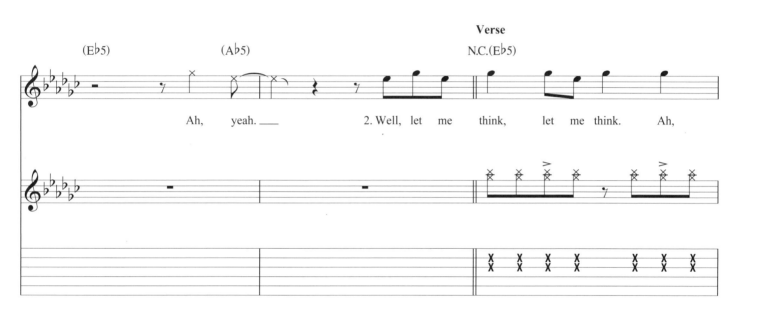

Ah,   yeah. ___   2. Well, let me   think,   let me think.   Ah,

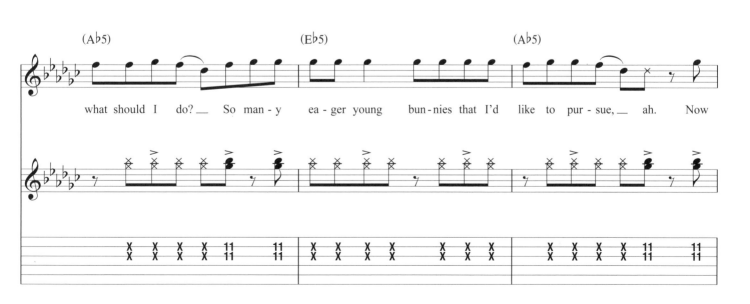

what should I   do? ___ So man - y   ea - ger young   bun - nies that I'd   like to pur - sue, ___ ah.   Now

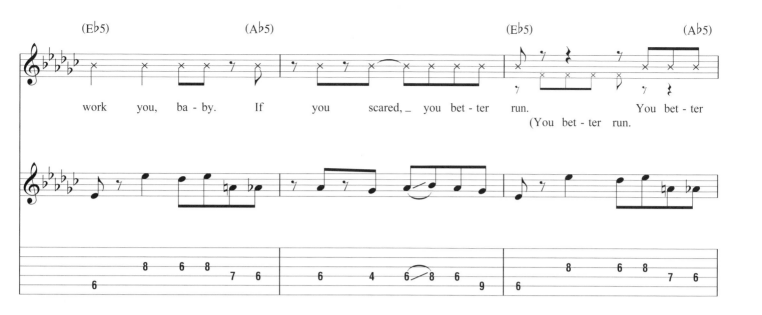

D.S.S. al Coda 2

⊕ **Coda 2**

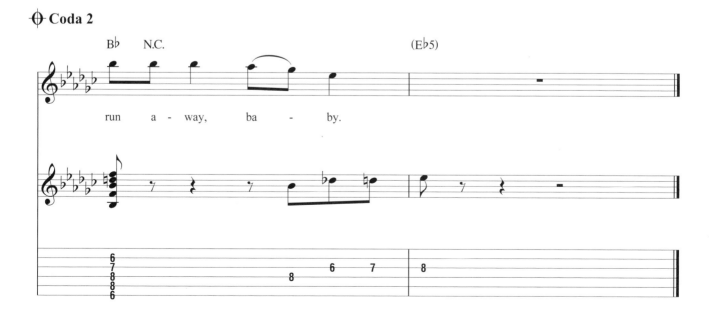

Treasure

Words and Music by Bruno Mars, Ari Levine, Philip Lawrence, Fredrick Brown and Thibaut Berland

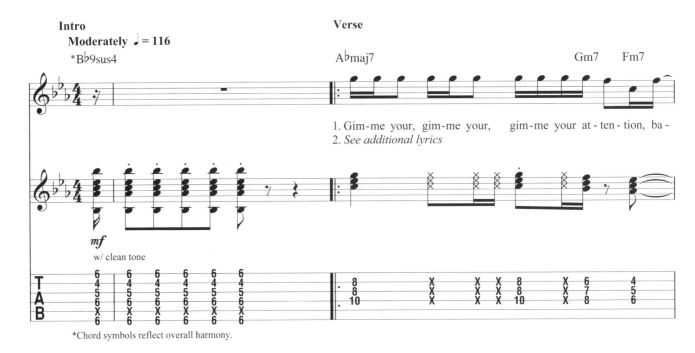

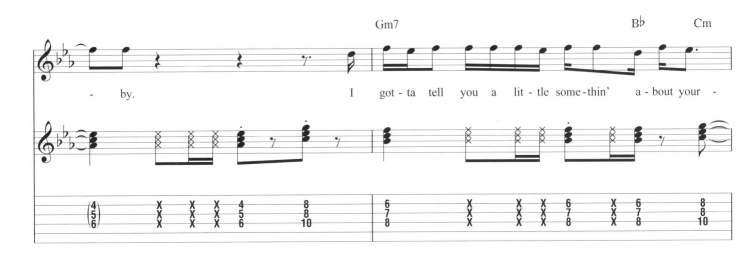

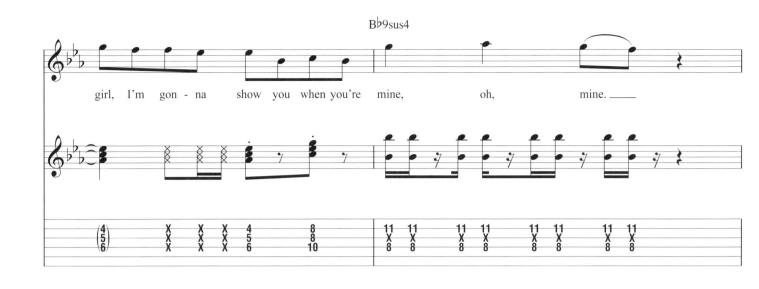

girl, I'm gon - na show you when you're mine, oh, mine. _____

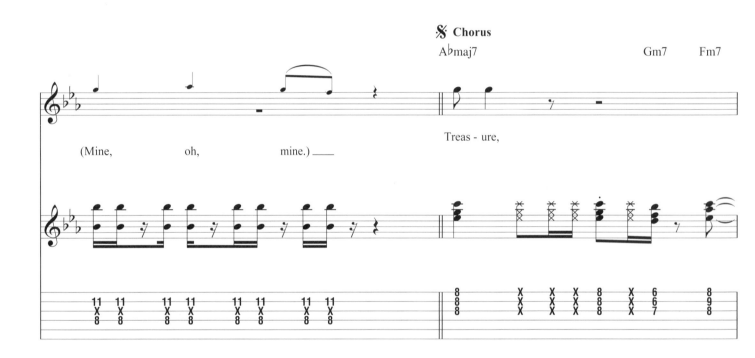

𝄋 **Chorus**

(Mine, oh, mine.) _____

Treas - ure,

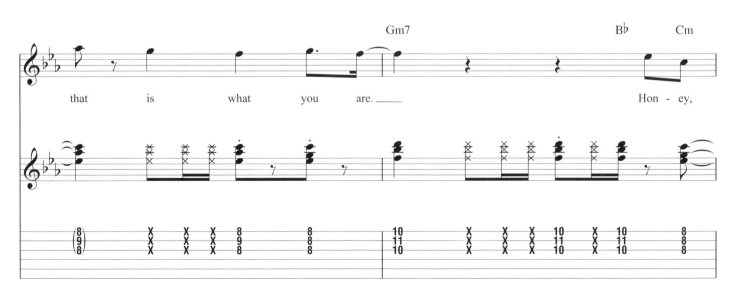

that is what you are. _____

Hon - ey,

Interlude

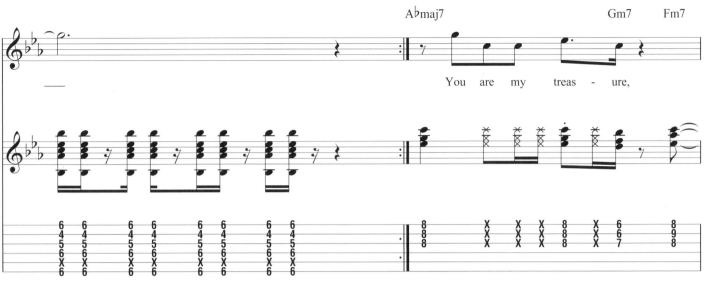

You are my treas - ure,

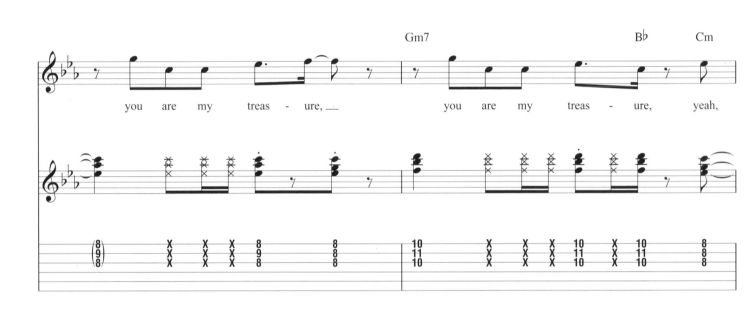

you are my treas - ure, ___ you are my treas - ure, yeah,

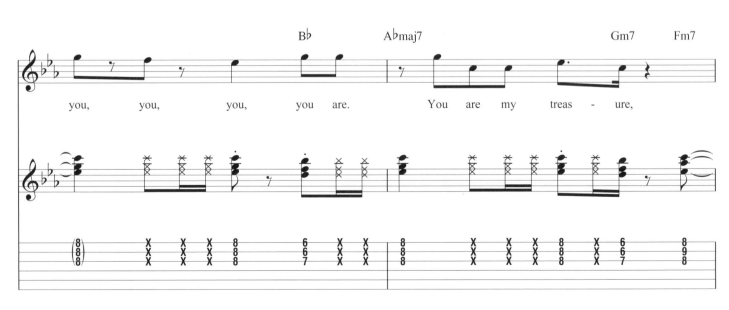

you, you, you, you are. You are my treas - ure,

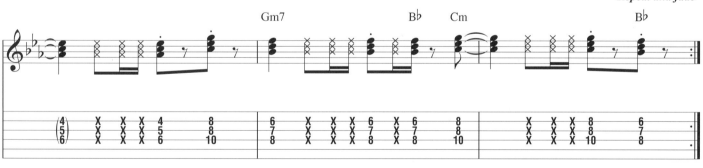

Additional Lyrics

2. Pretty girl, pretty girl, pretty girl, you should be smilin'.
A girl like you should never look so blue.
You're everything I see in my dreams.
I wouldn't say that to you if it wasn't true.
Oh, whoa.
I know that you don't know it, but you're fine, so fine.
(Fine, so fine.)
Oh, whoa.
Oh, girl I'm gonna show you when you're mine, oh, mine.
(Mine, oh, mine.)

GUITAR NOTATION LEGEND

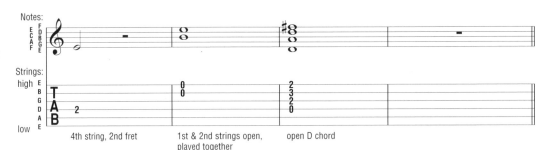

Notes:

Strings:

high E
B
G
D
A
low E

4th string, 2nd fret | 1st & 2nd strings open, played together | open D chord

THE MUSICAL STAFF shows pitches and rhythms and is divided by bar lines into measures. Pitches are named after the first seven letters of the alphabet.

TABLATURE graphically represents the guitar fingerboard. Each horizontal line represents a string, and each number represents a fret.

HALF-STEP BEND: Strike the note and bend up 1/2 step.

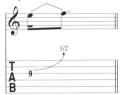

WHOLE-STEP BEND: Strike the note and bend up one step.

GRACE NOTE BEND: Strike the note and immediately bend up as indicated.

SLIGHT (MICROTONE) BEND: Strike the note and bend up 1/4 step.

BEND AND RELEASE: Strike the note and bend up as indicated, then release back to the original note. Only the first note is struck.

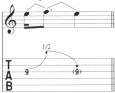

PRE-BEND: Bend the note as indicated, then strike it.

VIBRATO: The string is vibrated by rapidly bending and releasing the note with the fretting hand.

PALM MUTING: The note is partially muted by the pick hand lightly touching the string(s) just before the bridge.

HAMMER-ON: Strike the first (lower) note with one finger, then sound the higher note (on the same string) with another finger by fretting it without picking.

PULL-OFF: Place both fingers on the notes to be sounded. Strike the first note and without picking, pull the finger off to sound the second (lower) note.

LEGATO SLIDE: Strike the first note and then slide the same fret-hand finger up or down to the second note. The second note is not struck.

SHIFT SLIDE: Same as legato slide, except the second note is struck.

TRILL: Very rapidly alternate between the notes indicated by continuously hammering on and pulling off.

TAPPING: Hammer ("tap") the fret indicated with the pick-hand index or middle finger and pull off to the note fretted by the fret hand.

NATURAL HARMONIC: Strike the note while the fret-hand lightly touches the string directly over the fret indicated.

PINCH HARMONIC: The note is fretted normally and a harmonic is produced by adding the edge of the thumb or the tip of the index finger of the pick hand to the normal pick attack.

TREMOLO PICKING: The note is picked as rapidly and continuously as possible.

VIBRATO BAR DIVE AND RETURN: The pitch of the note or chord is dropped a specified number of steps (in rhythm), then returned to the original pitch.

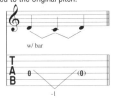

VIBRATO BAR SCOOP: Depress the bar just before striking the note, then quickly release the bar.

VIBRATO BAR DIP: Strike the note and then immediately drop a specified number of steps, then release back to the original pitch.

Additional Musical Definitions

(accent) • Accentuate note (play it louder).

(staccato) • Play the note short.

D.S. al Coda • Go back to the sign (%), then play until the measure marked "*To Coda*," then skip to the section labelled "**Coda.**"

D.C. al Fine • Go back to the beginning of the song and play until the measure marked "*Fine*" (end).

Fill • Label used to identify a brief melodic figure which is to be inserted into the arrangement.

N.C. • Harmony is implied.

• Repeat measures between signs.

• When a repeated section has different endings, play the first ending only the first time and the second ending only the second time.